AF605155

QUEENSLAND

First published in 2025 by New Holland Publishers
Sydney, Australia.
newhollandpublishers.com

 A record of this book is held at the National Library of Australia.

ISBN: 9781760797805

Managing Director: Fiona Schultz
General Manager/Publisher: Olga Dementiev
Designer: Andrew Davies
Production Director: Arlene Gippert
Printed in China

QUEENSLAND

nab
40

Arabella
JEWELLERS
Arabella
JEWELLERS
JEWELLERY REPAIRS

LIFEGUARD

CITY
TABERNACLE
BAPTIST CHURCH

WHEEL HOUSE

BUNDABERG
ESTD RUM 1888
ORIGINAL
CRAFTED IN AUSTRALIA
UNDERPROOF RUM
700mL 37% ALC/VOL
BUNDABERG DISTILLERY
WHITTRED ST.QLD

THE AUSTRALIAN STOCKMAN S H

CITY OF CANBERRA

QANTAS
VH-XBA
OVERSEAS AIRLINE

PLEASE
SHUT
GATE

QUARTZ BLOW
LOOKOUT

Bird

ville

XXXX

50

QUEENSLAND

- The nickname for Queensland is the **Sunshine State**, and a person who lives in Queensland is called a Queenslander.
- The **Koala** is the official animal of Queensland, but 85% of Australia's native mammals and 72% of native birds are also found in Queensland.
- **Gayndah**, on the Burnett River, is the oldest town in Queensland and was first settled in 1849.
- With **1.853 million** square kilometres and a **13,347** kilometre coastline, Queensland is the second largest state in Australia.
- Queensland has five of Australia's eleven **UNESCO World Natural Heritage Sites** including the **Great Barrier Reef**.
- Popular food in Queensland is seafood, fresh tropical fruits and **macadamia** nuts.
- **XXXX** beer was established back in 1877 and is the local beer Queenslanders drink.
- Queensland boasts some of the oldest **dinosaur footprints** in the world.